Save Your Whole Village
with these Therapy Solutions!!
Thank You!! Dr. Jenn

Men Don't Like Kids!
5 Ugly Facts™
About Human Behavior
(A Human Behavior Guide for Everyday Humans)

What People Are Saying About Men Don't Like Kids! 5 Ugly Facts™ About Human Behavior

You've heard of "pop" psychology; now brace yourself for *Shock* psychology!

Jennifer L. Rounds-Bryant, PhD
Author, Men Don't Like Kids! 5 Ugly Facts About Human Behavior

5 Ugly Facts™ translates complex academic behavioral research into everyday language!

Patrick Flynn, PhD
Institute of Behavioral Research, Texas Christian University

This book clearly explains the reasons and remedies for issues that affect everybody! Every police officer should have a copy as a handy reference.

Steve Chalmers, BS
Chief of Police, Durham, NC

Such easy reading brings behavioral theories to life. The book is a must for all human service and social science students!

Sheara A. Williams, PhD
Graduate College of Social Work, University of Houston

5 Ugly Facts™ is an important reference tool for all human service professionals!

Clinton DuBose, MA
Drug Treatment Specialist, Federal Bureau of Prisons

Men Don't Like Kids!
5 Ugly Facts™
About Human Behavior
(A Human Behavior Guide for Everyday Humans)

Dr. Jennifer L. Rounds-Bryant

Publisher
Mental Health Solutions
P.O. Box 14413
Research Triangle Park, NC 27709-4413
www.5UglyFacts.com

First Edition
First Printing

Printed in the United States of America

ISBN-13: 978-0-9798600-0-3
ISBN-10: 0-9798600-0-8

Library of Congress Control Number: 2007934733

Dedication

This book is dedicated to my children, Jillian and Emmanuel, who inspire me to be my best self. My priceless network of parents, family, and friends — *you know who you are darlings* — share equally in the dedication because they help me to be my best self.

Acknowledgements

The seeds of this book were planted 17 years ago when I decided that everybody should have the information that social scientists have known about human behavior for decades. My mentor, Dr. Patrick Flynn, has deftly guided my career along the path of bringing "research to practice". This book serves as the next step in my goal to make behavioral facts easily accessible to students, professionals, and everyday people.

I would like to thank members of my network of family and friends for helping to nurture the development of this book with generous amounts of support and encouragement. Some of the many human service professionals in my network were asked to review each *Ugly Fact* to ensure that it was quick and easy to read and error-free. Ms. Felicia Watson and Dr. Penny McKenzie reviewed *Ugly Fact #1*. Mr. Clinton Dubose and Dr. Patrick Flynn reviewed *Ugly Fact #2*. Dr. Joyce Roland and Ms. Lyndsey Hall reviewed *Ugly Fact #3*. Dr. Lela Demby and Dr. Sheara Williams reviewed *Ugly Fact #4*. And Ms. Kesha Lee reviewed *Ugly Fact #5*.

Ms. Elnora Shields served as editor and Ms. Danisa Baker served as copy-editor for the entire book. Mr. Michael Slaughter and Mr. Steve Steele provided graphic design for the book cover. Dr. Trevy McDonald provided publishing guidance.

A Big Thank You To My Patrons

A big thank you goes to the following people who purchased copies of the book before it went to press. Their early tangible show of support gave me proof of the book's value and further inspired me to complete the publishing process. I will always be grateful!

Mr. & Mrs. Jerry and Denise Guerrier

Mr. & Dr. Darryl and Tamera Beasley

Ms. Mary Liverman

Mr. & Mrs. George and Monica Perry

Mr. & Dr. Darryl and Tedra Brown

Mr. Carl Burks

Ms. Velma Burks

Ms. Frances Burks

Mr. & Dr. Anthony and Sheara Williams

Ms. Sharon Elliott-Bynum

Ms. Thalia McQueen

Table Of Contents

Introduction

There are many facts about human behavior that people tend to ignore time and time again, and then wonder why they keep ending up in bad situations. The bad part about it is that these facts are well known both academically and practically, but most people do not like to talk about them nor remind others of them. I like to call these facts *Ugly Facts* because they deal with the stark truth that most people do not want to face. This is especially true when it comes to motivation behind behavior and matters of the heart. These facts are presented in this condensed form in order to provide the tools needed to navigate through this crazy, but predictable world of people.

People are always amazed by the crazy things that other people do and the crazy situations they create for themselves. The good news is, and there is always good news, that learning how to use what we know about human behavior can help people to avoid bad consequences or at least help people to see them coming before the circumstances have them by the throat.

Somebody said "forewarned is forearmed" and I am adding that forewarned does not always mean that behavior will change just because someone can see danger coming. I believe that it is important to talk about these issues even if the information does not change anyone's behavior. This way, at least, I can rest easy and give people a well-deserved

"I told you so" when they go ahead and do something foolish hoping for an outcome other than the one everybody - including themselves - saw coming from miles away.

Ugly Fact #1
Men Don't Like Kids!

The Take-Home Message

1. Men do not like the work of kids. Yet, they want close emotional relationships with their children.

2. Responsive caregiving is the key to emotional closeness with children.

3. Children benefit from all positive interactions with their fathers and father figures.

The Truth Of The Matter

Men Don't Like the Work of Kids

The first *Ugly Fact* is that men don't like kids – or more specifically, the work of kids! This is an important fact because it impacts so many things in life – relationships, marriage, family life, child development, workforce issues, and human services. To be sure, nobody wants to hear this. But listen up because it's time to hear the truth. Even though there is full court press aimed at non-stop human reproduction, from using sex to sell everything and limiting sex education, to supporting the myths of the fairy-tale wedding, the everlasting honeymoon, and the first of many perfect pregnancies, the fact remains that men don't like the work of kids.

Finding Men with Kids

Men are by nature very sexual creatures, and prefer to have consistent access to gratification. So, some even buy into the candy-coated group of fantasies that make up happily-ever-after, and all goes well for the happy couple…until the children arrive. One peek into the average home with children will scarcely find a man present. Among married households with children, there might be a man listed on the mortgage or the lease, but the likelihood is that he is no more present to the children emotionally or psychologically than in the household where the father is officially absent.

Instead, one typically finds an overwhelmed mother who is too tired from trying to single-handedly manage the children and the household to have much sex.

The Historical Account

When Fathers Ruled

It's a good thing that children are the domain of mothers because when they were the domain of fathers, they were routinely subjected to abandonment, abuse, servitude, and murder. Before 1800 (and even now in some places), it was not uncommon in various cultures for fathers to abandon or kill children because they were too expensive to feed or because they were too much trouble in general.[1] If children were lucky, they were kept around to be used for violence, sex, or slavery. Children were not seen as valuable because they could easily be replaced and they were very likely to die before they reached adulthood anyway.

Modern Childhood

Along with societal advances in such areas as democracy, industrialization, scientific knowledge, and the child savers movement was the advent of modern childhood in the United States.[2] Within the context of these forces, children were increasingly valued for their ability to translate the American sociopolitical structure into future generations. The strains of modern childhood can be traced back to the middle of the 18th century, in the years prior to the Revolutionary War. However, the phenomenon did not become common for most children until the middle of the 20th century, in the years following World War II. With their elevated position, children required more humane care, and that care was turned over to the second class citizenry: women.[2]

Modern Parenthood

Despite being the primary responsibility of their mothers, children are nearly as likely to be abused by men as by women, according to national child protective services data.[3] However, father figures are most likely to abuse children fatally.[4] How interesting it is that there is typically a public outcry when there is news of child abuse and murder at the hands of a mother. However, the same behavior reported at the hands of a father is barely news worthy these days. If it happens at the hands of a mother's boyfriend or a step-father, it might receive some press, but an outcry is hardly ever heard about children suffering abuse at the hands of a father.

The simple ugly truth is that raising children can be very stressful, especially for a mother with inadequate help. Therefore, the surprise should be that so many children reach adulthood essentially unharmed, rather than that their mothers sometimes seriously harm them before they do.

Why Talk About It?

Thinking about Parenthood

So, is the point of talking about this *Ugly Fact* to discourage people from having children? Great question! The point is to get people to think realistically about what it means to have children outside of the cultural pressures for every adult to at least consider becoming a parent, and outside of the consequences of inconsistent contraceptive practices. There is a stark reality about the sheer difficulty of turning over oneself to the upkeep of an insatiable and mainly helpless human being that few people like to think or talk about.

The Realities of Gendered Role Expectations

One thing is certain for mom: the lion's share of the responsibility for child care will fall squarely in her lap, regardless of what other responsibilities she might have.[5,6] Dad can get away with blaming it on biological necessity and maternal urges for the first three years. But after mom has been in a sleep-deprived stupor for five years, there really is no excuse that dad can use to justify why he will fail to take an active role in Johnny's life for the next 13 years.

Now dad will point out that he plays with Johnny, pays for his upkeep, and even baby sits him when mom leaves the house in a stress-induced rage. So mom will have to give dad his credit. But it might be awfully hard to ignore the fact that mom is the one who does everything else for Johnny, outside of the things that dad can name so proudly!

Parenthood As Depicted In Popular Culture

The View from the Lens of Reality Television

All it takes is a look at the reality television shows which feature parenting issues to find married mothers who are overwhelmed from single parenting and fathers who have checked out of parenting both emotionally and psychologically! Both mothers and fathers have that look on their faces which screams "What have I gotten myself into?" Research substantiates the overwhelming and stressful experience of parenthood, specifically for women who are primarily responsible for child care.[5] The television shows illustrate how men, apparently not wanting to be impacted by their wives' trauma, either stay away from home as much as they can with work or some other worthy excuse, or they come home and either hide out or yell a lot to make everyone miserable.

A Particular Episode: The Close-Up View

A memorable episode of reality parenting television gave the audience a great example of this situation. The episode highlighted a father who worked at home in a basement office while mom was left alone upstairs all day to deal with four unruly children. Dad would get up early every morning, get himself dressed, get his breakfast, and then go directly into the basement. Dad made no attempt to assist mom, who was responsible for getting two children ready for school and then preparing to take care of two younger children while she attempted to clean the house all day.

The punch-line to the situation came when, precisely at noon, dad appeared from the basement expecting a prepared lunch. On the day of taping, mom did not have the luxury of preparing lunch in the midst of her active children and endless amounts of house work. When he saw that there was no meal, dad proceeded to berate mom about not managing her demands well enough to prepare his lunch as expected.

As is typical, the parenting expert was called in to provide on-site coaching to help dad understand that mom was not his hired help and that she was overwhelmed with the responsibility of parenting the children alone. The great thing about these shows is that television magic usually results in the parenting coach convincing dad to engage first with mom and then with the children in order to bring order to the household. Once mom and dad are united in their efforts and armed with a few tried-and-true parenting techniques, the children typically get in line with their parents' new behavioral program, all in about an hour. If only such television magic were available in real life!

Fathers As Protectors And Providers

What the Research Says

Although fathers do not typically embrace the role of direct caregiver, let's take a look at their role as family protectors and providers. Research tends to identify history, socialization, and gender roles as the reasons that men stay away from the hard job of direct caregiving.[5,6] Some research indicates that men have traditionally been the breadwinners and protectors of the family, leaving children to the care of their mothers. The notion is that more recent societal changes have lead to increased demand for father involvement beyond their traditional role because women are working outside the home in greater numbers.

What the Statistics Say

More recent societal changes do not erase the long history of poor and minority women in the workforce. Further, research statistics show that 30% of Caucasian, 42% of Hispanic, and 69% of African-American children are born to single mothers.[6] These numbers alone defy the logic of the wholesale branding of men as breadwinners and family protectors when many do not reside with the families they created.

What the Everyday People Say

Although many fathers do not marry their children's mothers, let's be sure to consider the absent married fathers. A cursory review of the history of adults raised with a father in their homes commonly results in the overall comment – "he was there…but he wasn't". Many people describe a father who worked most of the time, was tired when he was home, and was relatively uninvolved in his children's lives.

Even a modern-day peek into non-televised reality reveals a preponderance of married men who do not bother themselves with the day-to-day chores of changing diapers, feeding children, bathing babies, doing homework, van pooling to soccer practice, attending parent-teacher conferences, and taking children to doctor's appointments and birthday parties.[6] The daily drudgery of child care tends to fall on mom today just like it has since the advent of modern childhood. Whether it is fair or not, it is likely that these traditional gender roles and societal expectations – whether or not they apply logically to a specific man or woman – are responsible for men's typical limited involvement in direct child care.

Back to the Research

It would also be easy to say that men would be more involved if they knew the difficulty of direct child care. In fact, the research shows that dads do know how hard direct child care is for moms. Research indicates that mothers provide more direct care for infants and children than fathers, regardless of parents' education and income, children's ages, or mothers' employment status.[7,8,9] Further, a review of studies published from 1992- 2002 indicated that women find the first year of parenthood very stressful. Mothers report being overwhelmed with the constant care that children require, which leaves them with little room for rest or self-care, and wondering about their parenting skills despite their best efforts.[5]

Fathers expressed no overwhelming concern about the mother's strain with being the child's primary caregiver. Instead, fathers responded to this scenario by being concerned about their own parenting skills, complaining about not feeling close to the child for whom the mother is spending so much time administering direct care, and taking refuge in the safety of the role of protector and provider for the family.[5]

A Word for Mothers

How interesting it is that fathers rarely extend their perception of their role as protector and provider to include protecting the health and sanity of the mothers who bore the children and now have to expend considerable physical and emotional effort caring for them. Mothers are often puzzled about how a man who is supposed to love her, and certainly love his child, can witness the drudgery and burden of caregiving and not make a consistent effort towards helping to bear the burden. The reason is because there is nothing attractive about holding, feeding, and comforting a baby non-stop, both day and night. This work is best left to the frontline: mothers.

Mothers would do well to remember that most men are competitive, and that competition tends to engender one-up and one-down positioning. In contrast, women are mainly relational, which tends to encourage working together to engender positive team spirit and a win-win outcome. When a competitive person and a relational person are involved in a project which causes a constant drain on both time and energy, the competitive person is going to quickly figure out how to minimize participation in the drudgery of battle, while sharing equally in the spoils of victory. The relational person is going to look towards her team members to share both the work and the cake, so that everyone survives in a win-win fashion.

With a competitive person as her primary team mate, the relational person is poised to bear the lion's share of the burden of meeting the excessive demands of direct child care. In fact, some dads communicate to moms that they will not provide direct child care by asking the question "If I do that, then what will be left for you to do?" – or some variation. This common question has been infuriating to more than a few mothers because it suggests that there is some possible ending to the never-ending job of child care.

The Secret To A Close Relationship With Children

Responsive Caregiving

While most fathers have actively figured out how to avoid direct caregiving, they unexpectedly find themselves disappointed because they don't share the kind of emotional closeness with their children that their children seem to share with their mothers. What men don't understand, and what can be easily overlooked by overwhelmed mothers, is that the real spoils of victory come to the person(s) providing direct care to the child. Attachment Theory tells us that the real secret is this: the essentials of developing emotional closeness with a child require responding to the child's basic physical and emotional needs, on the child's cues, consistently and predictably.[10]

Meeting Children's Needs on Their Terms

While fathers are typically happy to play and interact with children on the father's terms (when he's home, when he's not too tired, and when he feels like it), children prefer caregivers who respond to them on their terms, at least initially. For example, a wet, hungry baby who needs some human closeness wants to be changed, fed what she customarily eats, and held in a way that is comfortable for her, immediately.

Satisfying a child's basic needs rarely coincides with an adult's schedule for these same needs. To be sure, responsive caregivers tend to make schedules for caregiving, but the schedule tends to develop based on the natural demands of the baby. This remains true even as children age and are subject to external time constraints such as school schedules and the like.

Wild about Mommy

Being such a responsive caregiver, it is no wonder that children are wild about mommy! Moms (and dads to be sure) are often mystified by children's preference for them, to the near exclusion of everyone else. For example, most moms can point out a time when a child has stopped playing with his father to go and ask mommy for a drink of water, something to eat, to show her a boo-boo, or some such request that one would make of a responsive caregiver.

When mom questions the child about why he didn't ask dad, the child generally retorts because he needed her. Dad usually chimes in that he would have responded if he had known. The answer to the mystery is this: when a child sees one person as a reliable source of comfort and sustenance, then the child is going to cling to that person for dear life.[10]

Any adult can relate to the fact that emotional closeness is built upon experiences we have with others who help us during our time of need. To be sure, needing a bottle or a bandage qualifies as a time of need every time for every child. When a child views a person as his playmate, or as a supplement to his primary caretaker, then the child will seek the person out mainly for play, and perhaps caregiving when his primary caregiver is unavailable. But oh boy, when the primary caregiver is available and the child needs something, the child will go straight to the source!

Bringing Dad into the Direct Caregiving Game

Fathers would do well to take a more long-term view of just what the spoils of direct caregiving can be and then decide what they want their roles to be. If dad only wants to be the large-size playmate, then playing with his child, to the near exclusion of any other form of direct child care is the way to go. But for fathers who want to be true providers and protectors of their children, who want their children to look to them for their very survival, then getting down and dirty, tired and frustrated with direct child care is the way to go.[10] It is bound to be the greatest battle ever fought and the greatest victory ever won.

The children are the undeniable winners in the quest to bring fathers into the caregiving game. For the record, children benefit from any and all positive interaction with their fathers – hands down – no questions asked! For the fathers who just want to play, take heart in knowing that you are teaching your children important lessons in human interaction, self-control, and adventure-taking.[11] In this case, dad is the go-to-guy for swashbuckling entertainment when the pants are dry, the tummy is full, and the children are wide awake.

Both boys and girls learn important lessons about taking risks and stretching their emotional and physical skills by playing with dad, which they are very unlikely to learn with mommy. However, dad will need to contain his disappointment when the children go looking for mommy when he takes them beyond their limits, or they are benched with an injury.

Now adding direct caregiving to the playful role preferred by many fathers hits the sweet spot with children and their developmental health. Children get someone upon whom they can depend for their very survival, AND with whom they can have a rip-roaring good time. Having a close emotional relationship (the by-product of responsive caregiving) with their fathers increases children's intelligence and cooperative behavior, as well as their self-esteem and their emotional health.[11] These positive effects will carry over into their entire adult lives.

Be aware that many dads will be amazed to learn these facts. They will be astounded that they have all of this good stuff to give. Rest assured, these benefits are absolutely real, and the only costs are dad's time and willingness.

On A Positive Note

Dads Doing at Least Their Fair Share

This *Ugly Fact* would not be complete without giving voice to the fathers who do hang in there and try to at least do their fair share with direct caregiving; including those who do more than their fair share for their own and others' children. They are spotted regularly doing both drop-off and pick-up at the day care and school. He is coaching basketball and soccer teams, at the deep end of the pool with his child during swim team practice, and at the semi-professional baseball game single-handedly managing all the children who see him as father one way or the other.

He can be found in the yard playing catch with his son in the dark with his work uniform still on, in the restaurant with just the children, at the laundry folding baby t-shirts with the baby on his back, and helping out in the classroom to support his special-needs child. Although they are rarely seen in great numbers, if you part the sea of women with children, you can find an occasional dad working in the yard with his daughter, as well as a dad out with his step-children on their weekly date.

Dads in the Game - in Their Own Words

When these dads are asked why they left the parenting bench and stay in the game, they usually say that they want to be a more active father than was their absent or present father. When asked what the experience of being an active father is like, they agree that it is much harder than they thought it would be. They realize that it would be much easier to be hands-off like most fathers, but the rewards from the children and their moms are far greater than what they would get just sitting by watching the moms perish from the challenges of child care.

The positive and cooperative attitudes of these dads bode well for the health of their families. Sharing the stress by providing direct caregiving to the children and mutual parenting support helps to sustain the physical and emotional health of the children and both parents, and helps to strengthen the marriage or relationship.[11] This will in turn help the children to learn valuable skills to use in their own functional families, which they will create to raise their own emotionally-healthy children.

Summing It All Up

The *Ugly Fact* is that men have made it clear that they certainly do not like the work of children. This message is illustrated in history, everyday life, popular culture, and research. Despite their exquisite ability to avoid the burden of direct child care, dads still feel a void when they see that their children have a closer bond with mom.

Research highlights the importance of taking care of children on their own terms in order to develop a close emotional relationship with them. So, while dad easily allows mom to do the lion's share of child care, he usually does not realize that her responsive caregiving is creating the foundation for an emotional relationship that will last a lifetime. The good news is that children benefit from all positive interactions with dad, and dad can also experience considerable emotional closeness with his children if he chooses to get off the parenting bench and stay in the game.

Ugly Fact #2
Family Members Support Alcohol and Drug Addiction

The Take-Home Message

1. About one in ten Americans (age 12 years and older) is addicted to alcohol or drugs, so every family has at least one addict.

2. Family members often unwittingly support alcohol and drug addiction, thinking they are supporting recovery.

3. Treatment for alcohol and drug addiction works, but the process is slow and painful. Family members have an important role in the recovery process.

The Big Picture

Alcoholics and Drug Addicts Are Everywhere

Every family has at least one alcoholic or drug addict. Addiction goes everywhere we go, from the mailroom to the pulpit, and everywhere in between. Addiction is a top public health problem in America. It costs more than $400 billion per year in lost lives and wages, health care, motor vehicle accidents, social services, and criminal justice costs.[1,2]

For the last five years, research has indicated that approximately 10% (one in ten) of Americans (age 12 years and older) are addicted to alcohol and drugs.[3] This number increases dramatically among certain groups, like those in the criminal justice system, where the rates of addiction are as high as 70%.[4] Many people are surprised to learn that alcohol addiction accounts for the majority (e.g., at least 60%) of both addicted people and the cost of addiction.[1,2,3]

Cost of Addiction: Priceless

Although most people understand the cost of addiction to be enormous when represented in terms of estimated sums of money, the social cost of addiction is priceless. Addicts lose their jobs and families, children of addicts lose their homes and their parents, and family members lose the addict. The reason addicts appear to turn their backs on everything unrelated to their addiction is because alcohol and drugs hijack the brains of addicts and lead them to focus considerable effort and energy towards securing, using, and recovering from each episode of alcohol and drug use.[5] Relationships and normal role responsibilities take a distant second place to alcohol and drug use for the addict.

The Role Of Family Members

Family as a System

Family Systems Theory tells us that families are joined together as an emotional system so that anything that happens to one family member affects everyone in the family in one way or the other.[6] The goal of the system is to continue to function normally, even in the face of distress. In functional families, sources of emotional distress are identified, discussed, and solutions are applied to the problem according to the prescribed roles in the family in order to help the system maintain normal functioning.

Family Secrets

When secrets are kept or emotional turmoil is ignored, then the family system will do everything it can to function normally *around* the problem. This usually leads to a significant disruption in the family system because family members do not publicly acknowledge either the problem or the consequences of the problem. Therefore, typical family role responsibilities are shifted in order to route the system *around* the problem. For example, if a parent's drinking leaves her unable to properly care for the children but no adult in the family wants to address the issue head on, an older child might begin to operate in the prescribed parental role by taking care of younger siblings and other household tasks.[7]

Family Sacrifices

Within the context of the shift in roles, the family system will usually sacrifice the weakest member of the family (usually a younger child) in the service of making sure the family functions in the presence of the unspoken problem. In this situation, the weakest member is considered the problem in the family and any solutions are directed toward fixing that family member, instead of addressing the parent's addiction. So, whether family problems like addiction are acknowledged, hidden, or ignored, they take a heavy toll on the family.[7]

Family Support for Addiction

The heavy toll of addiction is compounded for family members (and close friends) because they think the addiction is their fault or that they can stop the addict from doing all the destructive things that addiction leads a person to do.[7] Along with every addict comes someone who works really hard to rescue him from the trouble he causes. The addict will look for as many ways as possible to continue his addiction without negative consequences.

Here is where unsuspecting loved ones come in handy. Because family members want to help the addict get a handle on his addiction, they often provide just the support the addict needs to continue his addiction. For example, wives and mothers are very good at keeping the addict's secrets about drug use, based on his promise to do better next time. They also give the addict money for necessities such as rent and light bills, but the addict uses the money for such necessities as drugs and paraphernalia.

When he gets caught drinking and driving, someone gets him a lawyer to try to reduce the charges. When she loses her job, someone will pay her rent so that she and the children will not be put out on the street. Because he might forget to pick up the children from daycare, he is not even on the pick-up list. Over and over we see the numerous ways that families find to help their loved ones remain addicted to alcohol and drugs in their misguided attempts to help.

Keeping the Addiction Alive

Often times the wife is the martyr in the addiction process, but the husband can also play this role for his wife. Working together, the parents can be a formidable shield for their addicted child. If you were to ask these family members what they would like to see for their addicted loved one, they would say that they want him to stop using alcohol and drugs.[5] They would be astounded by the fact that their behavior is helping to sustain their loved ones' addiction. Instead, they see themselves as trying to help, and generally do not understand that saving people from the natural negative consequences of their addictive behavior helps to perpetuate the destructive behavior.

Family Members Benefit from Addiction

Family members claim that they want their loved ones to get help. But that usually means that they want them to get help according to their points of view. One need only look at reality television that focuses on addiction to see that it is difficult to get family members to agree about what help should be obtained, even though most are not addiction treatment experts. The highlight of these episodes is when the parents or the spouse want to dictate the terms of treatment to fit their own comfort zone.

The *Ugly Fact* is that family members get something out of loved ones being addicted and are reluctant to give up the benefits of the addiction.[7] So often the treatment is undermined or sabotaged, even while family members might say that they really want their beloved to get better. Family members often play on the fears and uncertainty of the addict to interfere with treatment.

The wife who is playing martyr to her husband's addiction earns the award for self-sacrifice. She gets to see herself as the savior of the family by overcompensating for and hiding her husband's addiction. She also gets to control most things in the household if her husband stays high enough of the time. She gets to be the hero to her children because she is the only one they can count on to hold things together. [7]

Parents who give money to their children to get high so that they will remain at home get to feel needed by their children.[5] Parents who protect their children from the consequences of their alcohol and drug use get to feel that they are fulfilling their roles as parents. In families where both the parents and the children are addicts, there is a kinship in the shared secret between them.

A Real Chance to Recover

In order for addicts to have a chance to recover from alcohol and drug addiction, family members must give up the benefits that they derive from the addiction.[7] This often means that family members must face the pain of letting their family secrets out, of disappointing their loved ones, and of watching addicts face the pain of job loss, homelessness, and instability in order for them to gain sufficient motivation to try the path of recovery from addiction. This is a lot easier said than done, especially when children or long-standing family secrets are involved.

The Realities Of Initial Recovery

The Picture of Addiction

Even when family members do not support addiction and do not interfere with treatment, the reality is that it is very difficult to stop using drugs and alcohol when one is addicted. Addiction makes a person spend most of his time getting and using alcohol and drugs; and makes him need more and more of the alcohol or drug to get the same high. It also makes him need the alcohol or drug in order to avoid physical and psychological withdrawal symptoms such as shakes, vomiting, and paranoia.[8]

It is important to understand that long before addiction occurs, the person has made the substance a central part of his life. He spends the majority of his time getting, using, and recovering from using drugs and alcohol. Asking the addict to give up her drug of choice is asking her to give up perhaps the most important thing in her life. If she started using drugs and alcohol as a kid like most addicts, she sees quitting as giving up the only reliable comfort she has ever known, embracing the pain of withdrawal, and facing the fears of living life without the comfort of alcohol and drugs as a buffer. That's an awful lot to ask of anybody.

By the time addiction is discovered, it has usually been developing over a long period of time, typically since the person's childhood.[5] Similarly, it takes a long time to recover from addiction. The normal process of recovery is predictable, starting first with seeing the behavior as a problem, deciding to do something about it, seeking the help needed, and then persisting in the changed behavior even in the face of overwhelming temptation. The fact is that recovery consists of multiple treatment episodes (or attempts to quit alone) and multiple relapses over a long period of time.[5]

Seeing the Addiction as a Problem

It takes most addicts a very long time to see their behavior as a problem[3] – this is the crux of the whole issue of denial. People are often frustrated by the fact that addicts rarely see a problem with their behavior, no matter what bad experiences have resulted. This delay in seeing the problem is supported by loved ones rescuing the addict from the natural consequences of his negative behavior.

The sooner an addict can have a bunch of meaningful negative consequences related to his addiction, the sooner he will see his addiction as a problem, if only for himself. This is why addicts who are coerced into treatment by their employers (to keep their jobs), the criminal justice system (to stay out of prison) or by social services (to regain custody of children) do just as well, if not better, than those who come to recognize the problem on their own and seek treatment.[9]

Reasons for Going to Treatment

It is important to note that family members rarely have the power that the court has to induce addicts to attend treatment. So, family members would do well to free themselves of the notion that they have the final say in convincing their loved ones to go to treatment. While family members can and should refuse to continue helping addicts in their addiction, their decision might not lead their loved ones to treatment.

Be clear that those who go to treatment because of a court order must still make up their minds to do the work involved in treatment in order for it to be effective.[9] However, it is often easier to give in to treatment when the long hand of the law has a say in one's life than it is to come to that voluntary decision on one's own. Once in treatment, the addict has to travel the long road of self-review on the way to the uncertain place of self-honesty.

The addict has spent a lifetime developing a distorted sense of himself and his reality, due both to substance use and to the need to see himself as different from his reality. Convincing himself to take a close look at his reality is the first step in a long journey that gets much more painful before it gets better. The recovery process involves the deconstruction of the addicted self and the construction of the non-addicted self.

The Treatment Process

Treatment typically lasts from a few weeks to a few months, depending upon the program and the funding resources. The prescription for research-based treatment usually involves outpatient cognitive-behavioral group therapy which meets for one and a half to two hours at a time, 1-3 times per week, and participation in self-help groups most days per week.[7]

Treatment will probably be more intense in the beginning, with group therapy at least 3 times per week and a self-help meeting every day for the first 90 days. What happens in group therapy is the foundation of the formal treatment experience. It is here that various topics related to the addiction experience are discussed. The group of addicts shares their experiences with a focus on exploring their thoughts and emotions and providing support to each other.

Focus on Group Therapy

It is a necessity for addicts to be honest in the group therapy process if they are going to really benefit from the treatment process. The professional facilitator typically asks questions and makes observations about what group members say to help the group to become more and more honest with themselves and each other. There is a focus on talking about feelings and taking the perspective of others in order to expand their understanding of the negative impact of the addiction on themselves and on other people.[7]

As can be imagined, this is an intense experience, pressing the group members to uncover what they have worked so hard to cover up for so long. What they discover about themselves in the process typically flies in the face of all the lies they have told themselves about themselves and their addictive behavior. Therefore, the process is very much like having well-tended scabs ripped off their egos, without the old comforts of alcohol and drugs to soothe or cover the excruciating pain!

Exposed: The Next Step

After exposing herself for whom and what she is, the addict gets to decide whether she wants to continue to be the person she has discovered. The value of seeing the reality of oneself is that one can decide to change or not. If the addict decides to change, then she has to draw on any previous experience she has had with being the person she wants to be (e.g., childhood experiences, values, skills) and learn the skills needed to reach her new goals. This generally involves continuing with honest self-discovery, obtaining medical care for medical conditions related to her addictive behavior, continuing her education, obtaining employment, working towards repairing damaged relationships, reestablishing housing, and regaining custody of her children, to name a few things.[7]

Rehabilitation Versus Habilitation

Assuming the adult roles that most people work up to gradually is typically the goal for most people in recovery. Here is where the distinction between rehabilitation and habilitation can be made. For those who have a history of positive functioning in their childhood and adult roles prior to their addiction, the goal is to restore them to their positive functioning – this is called rehabilitation. Unfortunately, most addicts have a very limited history of positive functioning, so the goal is to help them to develop the skills needed to function at an age-appropriate level – this is called habilitation.

The Work of Recovery

Recovery looks like a lot of work, and it is a lot of work. It requires a great deal of positive support from the people in the addict's social circle. This is where the importance of self-help groups is most significant. Fellowshipping daily with those who are living in the same community and facing the same challenges is as important for sustaining abstinence as treatment can be for initiating abstinence. Often, these self-help groups are the only form of intervention that most addicts ever get to because of a lack of health insurance and/or treatment options in their communities.[3] Self-help groups do not advertise themselves as formal treatment nor are they seen as such, but they certainly serve a vital role in the recovery process for many addicts.

Treatment Of Co-Occurring Mental Disorders

Addiction and Other Mental Disorders

Advancement in the understanding of addiction has revealed the importance of treating depression, anxiety, and other mental disorders at the same time as alcohol and drug addiction. Most people who have an addiction also have symptoms of depression, anxiety, ADHD, obsessive-compulsive disorder, and any number of other mental illnesses.[5,7] The symptoms of the disorders can be so intertwined that it can be hard to determine which came first.

Treating all Mental Disorders at the Same Time

The important thing is that all mental disorders are treated at the same time. [5,7] Although research supports this idea, and some treatment programs have successfully implemented dual treatment, the average treatment program is still treating addiction separately from other mental illnesses. Often these mental illnesses require the use of established medications, which goes against the tenets of most addiction treatment programs and self-help groups which focus on drug-free recovery.

Treating Addicts with Medications

The negative attitude towards treating recovering addicts suffering from additional mental illness with medication can create an awkward situation for someone who has suffered with depression her whole life and whose family is filled with people suffering from depression and anxiety. Her situation would suggest that the depression is part of her genetic structure and that genetic inheritance might have made her more vulnerable to addiction in the first place.

In such a situation, early diagnosis and treatment with antidepressants would have likely saved her a lifetime of pain and self-destructive behavior.[5] Further, treatment with antidepressants during the course of drug treatment would help to strengthen her recovery efforts. However, if she does not obtain treatment from a drug program which offers dual treatment, or does not seek the additional treatment on her own, she will continue to occupy the tightrope between mental health and mental illness, even if she manages to achieve abstinence from alcohol and drug use.

The irony to it all is that researchers have discovered medications to treat alcohol and drug addiction specifically. The medications interfere with the positive effects of alcohol and drugs on the brain, diminish the craving for alcohol and drugs (e.g., cocaine), and mimic or block the effects of illegal drugs (synthetic opioids and opioid-receptor blockers for heroin and other opioids).[5,10] These medications can give the brain an opportunity to recover from the effects of alcohol and drug use, and allow the addict to start thinking more clearly about the consequences of alcohol and drug use.

For example, research has shown that cravings can be activated by environmental cues related to alcohol and drug use in so short a time that the person does not even realize that the craving centers of the brain have been activated.[5] Medication helps to slow down these brain processes and allows the person to have more control of his behavior. As helpful as such medications can be in the recovery process, the stigma towards them is similar to that of more established mental illness medications (such as antidepressants). This is unfortunate for addicts whose brains have been hijacked by alcohol and drug addiction.

The Realities Of Sustained Recovery

Lapse Versus Relapse

Achieving abstinence is the beginning of recovery, and is typically the target of most treatment programs.[7] Sustained recovery is demonstrated over a period of about one year of more or less continued abstinence from alcohol and drugs. Because continued alcohol and drug use is an unfortunate reality of the recovery process, this behavior is categorized as a lapse or a relapse when it occurs after a period of abstinence. A lapse is defined as alcohol or drug use that occurs in a specific amount of time, and which does not reach the previous level of alcohol or drug use.[5,7] Relapse is defined as alcohol or drug use that occurs at pre-treatment levels

For example, a lapse scenario would involve Andrew, a recovering alcoholic. He has been abstinent from alcohol use for about a year and attends self-help group meetings at least once a week. His lapse occurs when he takes a drink at his sister's wedding reception to celebrate, and ends up getting drunk. The next day, he calls his sponsor to confess, attends a self-help group meeting, and returns to his alcohol-free lifestyle.

A Closer Look at Relapse

A relapse scenario would play out with a recovering crack addict (let's call her Nicole) who has gone to treatment, cleaned up her act, moved to another town, regained custody of her children, obtained her GED, and acquired gainful employment. Nicole comes back to town after a year in recovery to visit her family and friends. She hooks up with her old boyfriend, who offers her some crack to celebrate her success. She decides that she deserves it for working so hard for a whole year. Nicole reasons that it won't be a big deal…until she takes that first hit.

Because she has been abstinent for a long time, her brain experiences the high much more intensely than the last time she used it. Additionally, her brain is much more sensitive to effects of crack cocaine as a result of her previous addiction than it was before her addiction began.[5,7] One hit, and Nicole is hooked all over again. She stays out with her boyfriend for the rest of the week that she is in town. She returns to her mother's house tearful and penniless. Her mother gives her money to return to her new home. But Nicole is back out on the hunt for crack as soon as she returns to her new home. It's not long before she smokes up everything, loses her apartment and her job, and her family has to come to rescue her and the children from the new place.

Needless to say that everyone is more than disappointed in her behavior, most importantly, Nicole. After six months on the street, Nicole is exhausted and out of resources. Understanding how they have supported her addiction in the past, her family has told her not to come home until she is ready to go back to treatment, in an effort to stop rewarding her addictive behavior. So, when she decides that she had enough of living on the streets, she misses her children, and she is ready to stop using drugs, Nicole returns to treatment.

As a result of her first treatment episode and her relapse experience, Nicole brings five strengths into treatment that she did not have the first time: a GED, one additional year of recovery and work experience, the skills to establish a drug-free lifestyle in a totally new location, and the undeniable proof that she can not handle using crack recreationally. These five assets will be of great help to Nicole during her next episode of abstinence and recovery.[7]

The Role Of Family Members In The Recovery Process

Family Members Beware

Because of the cyclical nature of recovery, the recovery process is also a place where unsuspecting family members can serve to aid and abet addiction. The excitement of having a loved one in treatment can totally overshadow the fact that recovery necessarily involves multiple relapses.[11,12] So, it is easy for family members to believe that one treatment episode will mean that their beloved is cured of his addiction. However, family members must remember that recovery is a long-term fragile process, and that they must be even more careful about the support they provide to their loved one during this process.

Providing a hot meal and springing for a movie every now and then is ok, but giving money or other items that can be traded for cash or drugs is not. It is often important to be mindful that addicts who are new to recovery are not in the position to make up to their families for all of the hurt that they have caused. Making amends is a sensitive process that it usually long-term, and family members can count on the fact that their loved one will not be able to repay them for their pain and loss.

Support Recovery Not Addiction

Significant stress, untreated co-occurring mental disorders, and lack of support and positive activities can all negatively impact the recovery process.[5,11,12] Likewise success and confidence in the recovery process can lead to relapse because of celebration or testing.[12] That's why it is so important that family members maintain adequate boundaries as well as realistic appraisals of the addict's behaviors. Above all, do not keep secrets and do not become personally invested in behavior changes.

Encouragement and support are valuable contributions, whether they help the addict sustain recovery or not. Treatment works and long-term recovery is possible, but the addict has to want to stop using drugs and alcohol and engage in the often horrific recovery process necessary for long-term abstinence.[12]

Summing It All Up

Addiction to alcohol and drugs is an all-consuming family condition. Addiction occurs when the brain is hijacked by alcohol and drugs, rendering the addict a captive of the addictive process. The *Ugly Fact* is that family members often unwittingly support alcohol and drug addiction, despite their best intentions. The support comes in the form of hiding the addiction and rescuing the addict from the natural negative consequences of his behavior.

Often the secrets are kept and the rescuing is done in the service of maintaining a normally functioning family system. The catch is that addiction disrupts the family system, whether it is acknowledged or not. Recovery is possible, but involves a lengthy process, which includes lapses and relapses. Family members have an important role in the recovery process, but need to be mindful that they do not fall into the role of supporting addiction while trying to support recovery.

Ugly Fact #3
People Do Not Change Other People

The Take-Home Message

1. People do what they do to gain pleasure and to avoid pain.

2. People change when *they* decide to change.

3. The process of behavior change is predictable and challenging.

Why People Do The Things They Do

Gaining Pleasure, Avoiding Pain

When people think about wanting to change other people, they often wonder why people do the things they do. The logic or the benefit of the behavior is usually lost on the observer, often leading the observer to try to change the other person's behavior. The answer to the question of 'Why do people do the things they do?' can be explained simply by the principles of behavioral reinforcement. People do what they do to gain pleasure and to avoid pain, period.[1]

Behavior increases when the consequences are pleasurable (e.g., earning a special reward) or they relieve pain (e.g., take away fear or worry). Behavior decreases or stops because it causes pain (e.g., is punished). So anytime someone does something that seems foolish it is because she is getting something valuable out of the behavior, even if other people can not see the benefit.

Reinforcement is Person-Specific

When talking about the principles of behavioral reinforcement, it is important to note that pleasure, pain, and punishment are person-specific.[2] This is critical because what is extremely pleasurable to one individual might not get another person's attention at all, and thus will not increase the desired behavior. Likewise, what is painful and punishing to one person might appear pleasurable to another person, and will not stop the undesired behavior. In order for positive reinforcement to increase behavior, it must be perceived as positive to the target person – no matter how it might be perceived by everybody else. The same holds true for the importance of punishment being aversive.

Power Does Not Equal Control

People often have power over the reinforcements and punishments that affect other people's behavior (e.g., parents, supervisors, significant partners). However, it must be stated very clearly that the *Ugly Fact* is that people do not change other people. Even if someone alters his behavior in exchange for positive reinforcement, it does not mean that behavior will be altered over the long-term or that the person has changed.[3]

Stable patterns of behavior develop over a long period of time, beginning in childhood.[4] People tend to be committed to the behaviors that they do over and over again. These, in fact, are the hardest behaviors to change. In order for people to change their behavior, they must have a made up mind to do so, a mechanism for learning the skills associated with the new behavior pattern, the incentive to engage in the new behavior over and over again, and the expectation that the old behaviors will continue to emerge even while they are incorporating the new behaviors into their lives.[3]

It is tough to consider that a person might temporarily engage in new behavior for specific reasons because most people like to fantasize about permanently changing other people. Some people like to think that if they are nice enough, mean enough, persistent enough, or patient enough, their target will start *and continue* to help around the house more, help with the baby more, stop spending so much time on the hobby, lose weight, stop playing video games so much, stop shopping so much, stop letting people take advantage of her – the list of behaviors to alter could go on and on. Against all odds, people hope to change other people's behavior even if they do not want to change.

Trying To Change Other People

Changing Significant Others

The fact that people do not change other people is not as straight forward as it seems because sometimes it is possible to manipulate someone into doing something new. A real or imagined significant other is often a favorite target of people who want to change other people. Indeed, significant others might act differently to gain the rewards associated with pleasing their partners and perhaps out of fear of losing their partners. For the really astute student of human behavior, a person might temporarily change her own behavior in order to try to change her partner's behavior.[1]

For example, a woman will often change her behavior to make her partner happy, looking for the security of keeping him around. This does not mean that her partner has successfully changed her. Instead, she has decided to give him what he wants so that she can get what she wants. As most men find out later, if the requirements to keep him around are inconsistent with her long-standing behavior patterns, then one day the woman will likely decide that the price of keeping him is too high, and she will revert back to her long-standing behavior patterns.[4]

Honeymoon Period as Temporary Change

People frequently temporarily change their behavior to receive immediate rewards from other people. This explains the honeymoon period that people experience at the beginning of most new situations (e.g., relationships and jobs). People are typically successful at engaging in a new behavior as long as it is easy to do. However, as soon as people face a challenge or a difficult situation in the new experience, the long-standing behavior patterns quickly emerge! So, people would do well to postpone forming an opinion about someone until they have seen the person's behaviors in stressful situations.

Other People Will Change…

…Or Not

A common thought is that the other person will change when…we get together, we move in together, we get married, we move, when the baby is born…you can fill in the blank with anything. While behavior change might occur under those very circumstances, the truth is that you should put your money on the likelihood that most people go essentially unchanged through life's many transitions. The fact is that people tend to meet life's challenges based on the deeply ingrained behavior patterns which are learned early in life. [4]

In other words, a person who is flexible and positive will always cope well and meet the challenges of life on life's terms. In contrast, people who are slow to accept change will always want life's challenges to conform to their terms. So, by and large, that inflexible selfish person will always be slow to change and will put himself first – regardless of the circumstances.

While it is tempting to believe that the demands of the new circumstances will bring out more desirable behaviors, the truth is that new challenges typically bring out an exaggeration of the established behaviors patterns.[4] So when the selfish person meets change such as moving in with someone, he will focus on how to get his way as much as possible, regardless of the circumstances. The fearful person will avoid the new baby with great excuses, but the person who embraces change will face the challenges of moving into the new house head on like he does everything else. So, instead of changing old behaviors, the new circumstances will bring out the worst of the old behaviors. In fact, this happens even when there is a concerted effort to change because old behaviors get worse before new behaviors are established.

...When They Decide

While people can change for the better (and worse), it is usually as a result of their individual decision to change. The decision to change is translated into actual behavior change through great effort and sacrifice, lots of painful feedback, and still more effort and sacrifice over a long period of time.[3] The persistence necessary to change behavior comes because the person has decided to change for their own reasons.

How People Change Their Own Behavior

Behavior Change Occurs in Stages

Research indicates that behavior change occurs in stages which people usually travel through a number of times before long-term behavior change occurs.[3] For example, in order for a person to begin to manage his weight through nutrition and exercise, or give up drugs, or stop working so much, he must go through each stage several times before the change becomes long-term. There are a number of theories and models of behavior change, and they all have a number of things in common. For the purpose of illustration in this *Ugly Fact*, let's look at the very popular Transtheoretical Model of Change (TMC). The stages of change as outlined in the TMC include Pre-contemplation, Contemplation, Preparation, Action, and Maintenance and Relapse Prevention.[3]

The Pre-Contemplation Stage – I am not even thinking about changing my behavior.

The Pre-contemplation stage is where everybody starts and where most people spend their entire lives with respect to adopting important behavioral change.[3] This first stage is commonly associated with denial, because people have no awareness of a need for behavior change. As the name suggests, people in this stage have not "contemplated" or thought about a need for changing their behavior.

The obese person does not see her weight as a problem, the drug addict does not recognize his addiction, and the workaholic does not see anything negative about working constantly. So, any appeal to a person to change his behavior while he is in this stage of change generally falls on deaf ears. No matter how persistent the encouragement, if a person does not see his circumstances as problematic, he is not going to even think about changing. In fact, a person in the Pre-contemplation stage can be an expert at pointing out others' problematic behavior in a superbly successful effort to keep her thoughts off her own problematic behavior.

The Contemplation Stage – Hey, maybe I should think about doing something new.

The Contemplation stage finds a person actually "contemplating" or thinking about his behavior and the impact it has on his life.[3] The obese person might start getting a clearer picture of what she looks like and how her weight is harming her health. She might briefly entertain what it would be like to be able to walk up one flight of stairs or to the mailbox and back without being winded. The drug addict might begin to notice all the time he is spending on buying, using, and recovering from drug use experiences. He might fantasize about what he would do with all the money he is currently spending on drugs, and he might begin to see how drug use is holding him in a dead-end job. The workaholic might start to notice how disappointed his children are when he misses one more birthday party, soccer game, or school recital. He might start to wonder about whether his working so much will guarantee job security, or whether having lost his marriage was worth keeping his job.

When a person is in this stage, someone else pointing out examples of the negative effects of his behavior on his life is not likely to win any points toward helping the person to decide to change his behavior. Instead, supporting her self-directed evaluation of the impact of the behavior on her life, while emphasizing her power to make choices, will provide the support the person needs as she considers moving into the Preparation stage. Here again, a person in the Contemplation stage can also present himself as the expert on reasons that others should change their behavior, to further distract himself from his own behavior.

The Preparation Stage – Let's see how this might work.

The Preparation stage sees the person begin to take steps to prepare to change.[3] The obese person researches information on the internet about nutrition and exercises, and takes trial runs of the behaviors necessary to lose weight. She purchases low fat substitutes for her favorite foods, buys sneakers and exercise videos, and she tries taking the stairs instead of the elevator at work a couple of times per week. The drug addict tries to cut down on the amount of drugs he uses a couple of days a week, calls the Employee Assistance Program at work to inquire about treatment, and tries to limit the amount of time he hangs out with his drug friends to a couple of days each week. The workaholic leaves work on time a day or two per week, shows up at a soccer game, asks for a meeting with his child's teacher, and spends more time thinking about his emotional needs.

The person in this stage is quite literally on the ledge with respect to jumping off into a new behavior pattern. She realizes the sacrifice that will be involved in starting her new behaviors because of the internal discomfort she has faced during the trial runs and the reactions that people have given her based on those trial runs. People in this stage need the gentle support of professionals, friends, and family to cope with the discomfort and the newness of the new behaviors.

This person is literally at the crossroads of trying a new behavior and renewing his commitment to his old behaviors. The focus of the support should be on seeing the difficulties of the new behavior pattern the way the person sees them, highlighting the positive consequences of the new behavior, and emphasizing the person's continued choice in the decision to do things differently. When a person attributes his behaviors (and the rewards of that behavior) to his own choices, he is more likely to make a commitment to the choice, which is more likely to lead to sustained behavior change.

The Action Stage – I will try this new behavior!

It can be shocking to realize that there are three stages before the action stage – and note that none of the previous stages includes anything about someone else forcing a person to do the new behavior. The Action stage finds the person actually doing the behavior that she started off not even thinking about, then moved to thinking about, and then moved to learning the information and skills needed to engage in the behavior.[3]

This is the stage where Mary begins to eat more fruits and vegetables and exercise three times a week to alter her weight. This fourth stage is where David stops using drugs and signs up for outpatient treatment, which he attends in the evening. This is where John starts to leave work at 5 pm on Mondays, Wednesdays, and Fridays of every week.

Although it takes passing through three whole stages in order to reach the Action stage, the action stage should be considered the most vulnerable stage of all. This is the stage where everyone (including all interested parties) gets excited to see new behavior and then begins to have expectations about the behavior – that it will last, that it will produce the expected results, and that the results will be produced quickly. This pressure alone can quickly scare anybody out of her new behavior. Add to this pressure the pain of doing the new behavior – eating low fat foods instead of the high fat foods that Mary loves so much –

and the discomfort of engaging in the new behavior – David telling unfamiliar people in a treatment program the gory details of his life – and at hand are the reasons for a hasty retreat into the comfort of known behaviors.

Returning to well-established behavior happens more often than not, which is why new behaviors are so vulnerable in the Action stage of the behavior change process. The fact is that most people stop doing new behaviors before they become permanent habits.[3] Therefore most people have to cycle through the stages of change a number of times before new behaviors become a routine part of their lives.

Maintenance/Relapse Prevention – Hey, this is working for me...except when it isn't!

If the person navigates through the Action stage long enough, he ends up in the Maintenance (or Relapse Prevention) stage. This is the stage where the new behavior becomes part of the person's usual routine.[3] The behavior becomes part of the routine when the person consistently receives enough pleasure from a number of sources for doing the behavior.

Mary consistently eats nutritiously and exercises regularly because she has more energy, has lost weight, manages stress better, feels better about herself, feels empowered to take on other challenges, gets compliments about how great she looks, and can fit into more trendy clothes, just to name a few benefits. David no longer uses drugs because he has found relief from his emotional troubles, has found pleasure in new hobbies, has found a better job because he can think more clearly and is a more reliable worker, can spend his money on more interesting items and activities, and he feels better about himself. John continues to leave work on time three days a week because he enjoys spending time with his family, is able to exercise more routinely, is more rested and can therefore think more clearly, has rediscovered old hobbies, and feels less stressed about work. Notice that nothing was mentioned about changing behavior to please other people.

Over time, most people find that they have breaks in the new behavior – or experience short-term (lapses) or long-term (relapses) returns to their old behaviors.[3] The more well-established an old behavior, the more effort, time, and attempts it will take to change it or to substitute a new behavior for it. Breaks in the behavior are almost guaranteed when there is overwhelming stress on the system. When people are overwhelmed by stress, they typically revert to their most well-practiced coping mechanisms – and they do this automatically. However, it is important to note that the build up of stress usually occurs over time – so lapses and relapses are preventable.

All three of the people in our examples might find themselves breaking away from their new behaviors under the build-up of stress. Mary might find that it is easier to pick up a burger when she starts coming home tired from work because of the stress of mass lay-offs at work, instead of baking a piece of chicken and making a salad. This concession leaves her feeling sluggish and more tired, so she starts to skip her exercise sessions. Instead of maintaining her new behaviors in the face of overwhelming stress, Mary gradually goes back to her favorite coping mechanism: eating high fat foods and curling up in front of the television with a high-calorie treat to make herself feel better from the assaults of the day.

Most people experience lapses and relapses on the road to permanent behavior change.[3] The longer Mary was able to keep her new behaviors going before the onset of the stress, the more likely she will be to catch herself before she slides too far away from the new behavior. Because she got so much benefit from her new behaviors, Mary might notice the absence of any number of them when she decreases her new behaviors. She might start to miss the energy that came with her new behaviors, notice that her clothes might start to get a little tight, or realize that her stress level seems to be continuously elevated. If she is able to get back on track with the new behaviors without stopping them completely, then Mary's break would be called a lapse. If she completely stops the new behaviors long enough to return to her starting point (e.g., weight, stress level, or energy level), then her break would be called a relapse.

You can probably imagine that it is easier to recover from a lapse than a relapse. However, the good news is that there are powerful lessons even in relapses. The more of them a person has when trying to develop a new behavior, the more likely the behavior will be maintained the next time through the stages of change.[3] Indeed, lapses and relapses are disappointing for everyone involved. However, if people can receive support through each stage of the change process, no matter how many times they go through them, they have a fighting chance at permanent behavior change.

Summing It All Up

It is true that people do the things they do because there is some benefit in it. There is power in reinforcement and punishment, but there is greater power in long-established behaviors. Therefore, there is no getting around the *Ugly Fact* that people do not change other people. People change when they decide to change, and they do so according to a lengthy process. A popular model of behavior change is called the Transtheoretical Model of Change, which involves five stages ranging from Pre-Contemplation to Relapse Prevention.

Pain and challenges are encountered all along the path to new behavior, especially at the Action stage, which makes it the most vulnerable stage in the behavior change process. In the Maintenance stage, new behavior patterns become part of the person's daily life, but returns to old behavior patterns can still occur, especially in the face of stress. However, the more time engaged in the new behavior and the more benefits received from it, the more likely a person will return to the new behavior pattern. While lapses and relapses can be painful to all interested parties, people typically emerge from breaks in their new behaviors with more understanding and greater skills, which increase the chances of permanent behavior change each time people travel through the behavior change process.

Ugly Fact #4
Domestic Violence Is An
Equal-Opportunity Killer!

The Take-Home Message

1.   About one in four American women experience domestic violence in their lifetime.

2.   For someone experiencing domestic violence, the situation typically does not change significantly in a short period of time.

3.   Children suffer from witnessing domestic violence as much as if they were experiencing it themselves.

What Is Domestic Violence?

Definition

Behavior is considered domestic violence when someone uses tactics such as intimidation, space violation, name-calling, threats, humiliation, pushing, shoving, elbowing, kicking, slapping, hitting, punching, poking, spitting, forced sex, financial control, social isolation, and any other behavior to dominate, control, and terrorize one's intimate partner.[1]

Prevalence

An estimated 26% of women (which is a little more than one in four) in the United States experience domestic violence sometime in their lives while involved in both heterosexual and homosexual relationships.[1] Although both genders can be victims of domestic violence, women are by far the most common targets of domestic violence at the hands of both men and women. This means that domestic violence touches women in all categories of education, neighborhood, income, family type, and any other group to be named.

Domestic Violence Kills Everything It Touches

Killing the Mind

The *Ugly Fact* is that domestic violence is an equal-opportunity killer because it kills everything in its way. It starts out by killing the mind of the victim. The victim stays freaked out, depressed, and worried, even when she acts like she's fine.[2] She looks great because she has to work hard to hide the fact that she is being abused. The fact is that at first she can't believe that someone is doing this to her, then she tricks herself into believing that he will stop if she can just get her act together. At least that's what he tells her anyway. So, if she can just make sure that everything is right with his world, then he will stop abusing her because he loves her...and he will love her to death if she lets him. So, since her mind tells her that he's going to stop, there is no need to tell anyone, get anyone upset, or risk the embarrassment of people knowing that she is being abused.

Killing the Body

Along with the psychological impact comes the physical damage: bruises, cuts, broken bones, black eyes, ripped out hair, and lots of tears. And all of this comes from the man who proclaims to love her so much. And he will love her to death...if she lets him. In order to protect her secret, she will try to fix her own injuries, hide them, or lie about them when they come to light. Above all else, she does not want to reveal her secrets or be embarrassed.

Witnesses to the Crime

As with any serious violent act, there are usually witnesses to domestic violence. These witnesses typically come in the form of small children. Research indicates that children are present at domestic violence events about half the time, and that about 81% of children witness their mothers being abused by intimate partners during these events.[3] So, the children also suffer the fear, depression, and secret keeping experienced by their mothers. It is important to realize that witnessing domestic violence of any sort can harm children for the rest of their lives.

Two Types Of Domestic Violence

Situational

While there is a general description of domestic violence, research notes that there are generally two categories of domestic violence: situational and chronic. Situational domestic violence tends to occur between partners occasionally during the course of conflict management.[4] For example, she might call him horrible names and punch him in the chest during an argument about his looking at another girl. And he might return the harsh names and push her down for refusing to stop screaming in his face.

In this exchange, the couple is typically mutually violent, and it occurs in an emotionally provocative situation. Neither person believes him or herself to be a victim of abuse. They would describe the situation as one that got out of hand, and describe it as happening only occasionally. In this situation, neither person would say that he or she is in serious danger or that the violence was used as a domination or control tactic.

Chronic

In stark contrast to the situational type, with chronic domestic violence, often called intimate terrorism, the abuse is typically inflicted one way, and it is for the purpose of dominating, controlling, and terrorizing the victim.[5] This is generally where he uses space violation, harsh name-calling, constant threats and undermining, along with punching and kicking to make her obey him and to stay close to him. Talk show guests routinely illustrate this process when they reveal that chronic abuse can escalate to dictating what clothes to wear, what to eat, when she can leave the house, when she can spend her own money, her friends, and anything else that he believes is necessary to keep his woman in line.

But let's not forget the man who beats his wife only occasionally because he keeps her so scared that he will hit her that he only needs to hit her once in a while to control her every move. We should also remember the alcoholic who only lashes out when he is drunk, and therefore keeps his partner terrified of when he will come home drunk. The *Ugly Fact* is that chronic domestic violence is deadly even when it is only occasional because even the fear of it happening kills the soul. While all interpersonal violence has its negative consequences, chronic domestic violence, which is the focus of this topic, is the form of domestic violence which is typically associated with long-term treacherous outcomes.

Perpetrators

Men Who Feel Helpless and Powerless

Research tells us that chronic domestic violence is typically perpetrated by a man who feels helpless and powerless in his own life.[4] He is afraid of intimacy, but feels dependent on his intimate partner. He is often scared to death of losing her to someone else because he does not think he is good enough for her. These feelings can arise from negative childhood experiences (e.g., physical, emotional, or sexual abuse), and often cluster together in personality disorders.

Need to Dominate and Control Partner

Perpetrators have the need to dominate and control their intimate partners in order to feel better. They hope to find relief from the insecurity they're drowning in by terrorizing their women. The paradox is that the violence does not really help make the perpetrators feel any better. In fact, it often makes them feel worse because it increases the chances of their greatest fear: losing their intimate partners. This creates a pretty vicious cycle of negative feelings – violence – fear of abandonment – more violence. Perpetrators may indeed feel sorry for their behaviors, but the need to control their women to relieve their internal pain far outweighs any regret they might feel and virtually guarantees that there will be a next time.

Why Domestic Violence Happens

Cultural Explanations

As with anything people do, there are various thoughts about why domestic violence occurs. Research on culture tells us that domestic violence occurs because social forces all over the world support male dominance – This is known as the Feminist Theory on domestic violence.[6] Stated simply, the theory asserts that men are in charge of the world, and women are not. Therefore, it is reasonable that men control women, and do it through violence when needed. This view is supported by the fact that domestic violence only became illegal in the United States with the inception of the Violence Against Women Act of 1994. Further, there are many places in the world where domestic violence against women is allowed by law.

Psychological Explanations

Psychological theories about individual characteristics that contribute to domestic violence focus on things about a person's thoughts and emotions, as well as his personality make-up. As discussed earlier, examples of thoughts and emotions associated with domestic violence include thoughts about being powerless and wanting to control one's mate, and feeling insecure and fearful about losing one's mate. Examples of negative personality styles related to domestic violence would be a wholesale focus on oneself at the expense of others, unhealthy dependence on other people, and poor impulse control.[7] These psychological and personality variables can easily translate into a chronic domestic violence situation.

Familial Explanations

Research on family dynamics tells us that domestic violence is a result of negative experiences in one's childhood family environment.[8] Research shows that domestic violence perpetrators come from families where there was domestic violence, child abuse, and addiction. The notion is that people learn to respond to conflict with violence in their childhood family environments by watching parents and other family members. Family dynamics related to domestic violence must also be considered within the environmental contexts of race, poverty, and religion, which increase or decrease the likelihood of domestic violence.

Women's Response To Domestic Violence

Gradual Onset of Domestic Violence

A woman's response to domestic violence can be as varied as there are women. The most typical response to being in a domestic violence situation is often shock and disbelief. The domestic violence process can start slowly with subtle attempts to dominate and control the woman by making hurtful or sarcastic comments designed to undermine the woman's confidence and self-esteem.[9] If the woman appears to accept these behaviors by not clearly demonstrating her objection, then the attempts to control her will increase until she feels like a prisoner in the relationship.

From the outside looking in, it is easy to judge a woman who finds herself being controlled by a man. People can clearly state what they would and would not do, and what they would and would not allow in situations they are not experiencing. However, very few women can deny putting up with and going along with certain things just to keep the peace with a partner, parent, boss, or even a child in order to maintain their sanity. The problem with going along with the perpetrator of domestic violence in order to keep the peace is that this indicates acceptance, which he sees as permission to escalate his control tactics.

Abrupt Onset of Domestic Violence

In contrast to a gradual onset, the domestic violence process can also start rather abruptly with physical violence at the onset of the process.[9] Again, the typical response to being pushed, shoved, slapped, punched, kicked, bitten, or spat upon is usually disbelief, followed quickly by denial and refusing to believe that it will happen again. These ideas are usually supported by the immediate apology and promises of the perpetrator. The woman is quick to believe his explanation about what happened and his promises to never do it again because she hopes that the perpetrator will stop the behavior as suddenly as it started.

In this situation, the woman might think that doing things just right will stop her man from abusing her again. But just like the situation that occurs gradually, any measure of accepting his behavior (e.g., going along to get along) will result in increased control tactics. Simply put, a man who has chosen to dominate and control his partner through the use of interpersonal violence as a way of coping with his own fears and insecurities will maintain this coping skill in his tool kit, even if he only pulls it out every now and then.

Difficulty Seeking Help

It is often very difficult for a woman to seek help, even when she realizes that she is deeply involved in a chronic domestic violence situation.[9] There is great embarrassment about admitting to being a victim of domestic violence, even now that domestic violence is a crime in all states. Like some men, some women grow up thinking that domestic violence is a normal part of a relationship. Also, women can often see how they contributed to the situation by accepting controlling and violent behaviors early on in the relationship.

Let's not forget to mention the real possibility of less-than-supportive responses of family, friends, and even law enforcement officers to women's reports of domestic violence. Therefore, even when it becomes clear that her partner is not going to stop the abuse and she is in fear for her life, it can still be very difficult to ask for help or to make the decision to leave. Add to this difficulty the promises and threats of the perpetrator to kill the woman and/or her children if she tries to leave, along with a lack of financial resources, and you have the perfect reason why a woman would appear to choose to stay in an abusive relationship.

Children's Response To Domestic Violence

Children are Silent Victims

Women are not the only victims of domestic violence. Children are typically silent victims as well, even when they themselves are not being abused. Research tells us that children are present in about half of domestic violence situations to which police are called, and that the majority of those children witness the domestic violence.[3] Witnessing domestic violence causes trauma that stays with both boys and girls throughout their lives.

Lifetime Consequences for Children

Girls who witness domestic violence often grow up to have poor physical health, suffer from mental health problems, to choose batterers for their intimate partners, and to perpetrate violence in their relationships.[10,11] Boys who witness domestic violence often grow up to be batterers in both their dating and marital relationships. Further, the majority of juvenile delinquents, who are mainly boys, report being exposed to domestic violence as children.[8,11]

Women (and men) often think that children are unharmed in domestic violence situations as long as they are not being abused. However, everyone would do well to realize the wholesale negative impact on children of even witnessing domestic violence and being continuously exposed to the stress of the effects of the domestic violence on their mothers. Although many women get the courage to leave their abusers when the violence is carried over to the children, many more generations of children could be saved from the negative fall out from domestic violence if mothers could act on behalf of their children at the first signs of domination and control tactics from their partners. There is something about protecting their children that can generate determination in women to seek safety that is not generated regarding saving their own lives.

Perpetrators' Response To Domestic Violence

Blames the Victim

Keeping in mind that men are violent with their partners mainly out of their own insecurities, then it is not surprising that a man typically blames the woman for his control tactics.[9] He focuses on her behavior as the reason that he is violent towards her. In his mind, it is reasonable that he should control his partner by any means in order to ensure that his insatiable needs for security are met. In order to keep her close to him, he establishes tight rules and expectations, which are often so unreasonable that she can not consistently meet them. When she fails to meet them, then the only logical response is to increase his controls, which generally includes violence.

Minimizes His Own Behavior

When the police or other human service agencies become involved, he sees this as a violation of his privacy and becomes angry about other people getting into his business. By the time his behavior is detected by outsiders, he is usually quite skilled at minimizing his own negative behavior, while exaggerating hers. Depending upon his skills of persuasion, the perpetrator can be very good at convincing others that his perspective is the truer perspective.

Response to Treatment

Even when he agrees to participate in a court-ordered treatment program, the goal is rarely to change his behavior. More likely, his intention is to convince everyone that his violent behavior is well within his rights. Barring this, then his intention becomes to falsely convince the treatment provider that he has learned his lesson in order to avoid further sanctions. However, as with any typical situation, there can be exceptions to the rule, with some perpetrators making good use of treatment to try to change their behaviors.

Domestic Violence Treatment Strategies

Court-Ordered Treatment

Being violated by her intimate partner is devastating to a woman and destroys any trust or real intimacy with the partner because of the uncertainty about when the violence will strike again. The victim is just like any other victim of violent assault, except she is intimately involved with the perpetrator. Although domestic violence is a crime, a typical response to the crime is court-ordered behavioral treatment because research shows that batterers may change partners, but they will continue to physically batter, often even with formal treatment.[8]

Treatment Based on Feminist Theory

The typical treatment model for male batterers consists of group therapy with a focus on victim empathy, anger management, and positive conflict resolution. Treatment is based primarily on the Feminist Theory explanation of domestic violence.[12] Couples therapy is sometimes used to address domestic violence which has not reached the attention of the criminal justice system. In this model, domestic violence is treated as a relationship power and control issue, and the role of each partner in the battering is closely examined.

Treatment Outcomes

While perpetrators can change, they do not change without sustained effort, hard work, and determination based on their own choice to do so. The vast majority continue to abuse their partners in one way or another even after court-ordered treatment.[12] They might stop hitting their partners, but they often continue with verbal harassment, social isolation, and other non-physical control tactics.

Helping Someone Who Is Experiencing Domestic Violence

Leaving is Not Easy

Considering the wholesale damage caused by domestic violence, the response to how to help someone experiencing domestic violence would seem to be obvious – to encourage her to get out and get out now! However, reviewing women's typical response to domestic violence is a reminder that leaving is usually not as easy as it would seem from the outside looking in. Therefore, the most important way to help someone experiencing domestic violence is to provide empathy and support. Assuring the victim that her concerns are real and helping her to develop a pathway out of her situation which is reasonable for her specifically, while placing no pressure on her to use it, can be very helpful.[9]

The Role of Human Service Agencies

There are human service agencies that serve victims of domestic violence in most communities.[9] These include telephone hotlines which provide information about domestic violence, crisis intervention, and information about services available to help women escape domestic violence situations. These agencies can provide a variety of services to adult victims, including transportation and temporary housing.

Homeless as a Consequence

In the face of imminent danger, many women take their children and leave their homes before they can gather resources or make a plan. Unfortunately, many homeless women and children are victims of domestic violence with no assets or other support, and consider it lucky to find space in a homeless shelter. Others are forced to make do with sleeping in cars and hospital waiting rooms, and the occasional temporary shelter from family and friends.

Going Back Home

In the quest to help victims of domestic violence as a professional (friend or family member), be mindful that even if a woman leaves her violent situation, the chances are great that she will return to her abuser time and again.[13] It is important to remember that she probably loves her partner and has high hopes that he will be different now that he sees she will leave him. In addition, she probably does not have the resources to care for herself and her children if she remains on her own.

While this situation can be very frustrating for the helper, the ideal goals of helping should be providing support through the crisis, and helping the woman to plan her response to the next crisis – and there will be another crisis if she returns to her abuser. Understanding this dynamic can help the helper to have realistic expectations about victims' response to help.[14]

Summing It All Up

The bottom line is that if someone is experiencing domestic violence, the situation will not change significantly in a short period of time. The *Ugly Fact* is that domestic violence is an equal-opportunity killer. Women decide to stay in domestic violence situations for all kinds of reasons, but they do so at the peril of themselves and their children. It is noteworthy that many women will stay as long as domestic violence is limited to them. However, when domestic violence spreads to their children, this often gives them the courage to leave. It is imperative that everyone understands that children suffer from witnessing domestic violence as much as if they were experiencing it themselves.

Unfortunately, although there are typically human service agencies in communities which offer help, women often believe that they do not have the social support or the financial resources to flee a domestic violence situation. Even when they do leave, these barriers typically lead them back home. Returning home typically results in tightening of the control tactics and heightening of the violence. These facts highlight the need for sharing information, social support, and crisis response planning as the primary ways to help someone experiencing domestic violence.

Ugly Fact #5
People Ruin Their Own Lives!

The Take-Home Message

1. People play a role in both the good and the bad things that happen to them.

2. People ruin their own lives by rewarding negative behavior towards them.

3. Taking the chance to act in their own best interest is the key to people creating the lives that they want for themselves.

The Choices People Make

Making Choices, Regardless of the Options

Living requires choices, which people make in every situation. In other words, people are required to play the hands they are dealt in life.[1] To be sure, people may not choose the hand they are dealt or the circumstances within which the game is played. But one can always decide how to play one's hand in any given circumstance.

Whether to stay and play or fold and go is always a choice, even if it does not appear to be so. This fact is often missed, and typically results in people seeming to stay to play, but actually checking out of the game and then wondering why things don't go the way they expected. Staying to play and being in it to win require conscious thought and consistent effort.[2] When either of these is absent, it is no wonder that a person's circumstances goes in an unexpected direction.

Making Choices, Ruining Lives

The *Ugly Fact* is that people ruin their own lives by the choices they make. Whatever is getting in the way of a person's happiness, take bets that the person is playing the biggest part in it.[1,2] People are experts at identifying how others cause their unhappiness. However, it is important to realize that each person plays the starring role in his own agony.

If people look closely enough, they can see beyond blaming everyone else, and realize that they are the principal source of most of the disappointment in their own lives. This ugly little fact means that everyone can take responsibility for his own happiness. And science tells us just how to do this!

Assigning Responsibility

Why it's Someone Else's Fault

People see others as the cause of their problems because it is far easier to point the finger at someone else, and therefore hand over the responsibility for an unfulfilled life to that someone else.[3] For a person to accept personal responsibility for pain would require him to face the fact that he is ruining his own life, and consequently that he is responsible for saving the life that he is killing. This may be hard to accept and even harder to do, especially if there is a worthy scapegoat available.

Identifying a Scapegoat

That scapegoat is usually a person's closest associations. Spouses often blame each other for dashed dreams and missed opportunities. Parents often blame their children, and siblings often blame each other or their parents for circumstances being less than what was expected in their family life. Turning to negative circumstances on the job, let's not leave out the mutual blame between employers and employees, and the collective finger-pointing at corporate heads.

Research shows that people are more likely to take credit for positive outcomes in their lives and to blame outside forces for negative outcomes.[4] This is one way that people maintain a positive view of themselves. So, if a person's life is going well, then she is very likely to give herself credit. However, if things are not going so well, then he is very likely to attribute that to things outside of himself - mainly other people and perhaps uncontrollable circumstances - in order to preserve his positive image of himself. While this is definitely a good strategy for the short-term goal of maintaining a good view of oneself, in the long-run, the strategy robs a person of his power to change his behavior in order to improve his life.

The Role of Reward and Punishment In Ruining People's Lives

Rewarding Desirable Behavior, Punishing Undesirable Behavior

Consistent with the idea that people are responsible for their own happiness, behavioral research tells us that the most reliable way to alter our surroundings is to change our response to those surroundings. For example, behavioral research tells us that providing consistent rewards (positive reinforcement) for desired behavior and punishment for undesired behavior is the most effective and efficient way to manage and train children to be cooperative and companionate much of the time.[5] One needs to watch only one or two episodes of the popular reality parenting shows to see this in action. Although parents like to blame their children for their children's negative behavior, the parenting coach of the hour usually brings the parents around to understanding that the children persist in their negative behavior because the parents – mostly the mother because the father is usually uninvolved in the day to day parenting – reward the children for negative behavior, and often ignore or punish positive behavior.

In fact, the application of rewards to increase desired behavior and the application of punishment to decrease or eliminate undesirable behavior is relevant to every behavior. Simply stated, people are programmed to do those things that bring rewards and to avoid those things that bring punishment. The system of reward and punishment guides human behavior even when we are not aware of it.[5]

Rewarding Undesirable Behavior, Punishing Desirable Behavior

People often complain about how someone mistreats them without realizing the role they play in helping the person to mistreat them. More specifically, it is easy for people to fail to see how they reward others for mistreating them. This lesson is lost on people time and again, even as they reward others for mistreating them in multiple areas of their lives – relationships, work, and social situations.

For example, people at church ask Mary to do something she really hates to do, so she rewards them for asking her by agreeing to do it just once. As expected, Mary does a fabulous job, and then she gets mad when her church members keep asking her to do the activity, without realizing that she continues to reward them by doing what they ask – "just one more time". Similarly John rewards people for overwhelming him with responsibility at work because he continues to show up as the "go to guy".

In her management position, Ann rewards people for doing shoddy work by removing work responsibilities from them or not assigning it in the first place, and then she gets mad because she has so much work to do herself. The result is that Ann has surrounded herself at work with people who do not do well thinking for themselves but whom she can control. Then she gets mad when they do not take any initiative to do things on their own. When they do take initiative, Ann punishes them by reprimanding them for not executing their work flawlessly, instead of rewarding them for the effort and then providing additional coaching.

Most of the time people reward others for mistreating them because they are afraid that people won't give them what they need (e.g., acceptance, attention, love) if they do not do what others want them to do.[6] So instead of refusing to allow themselves to be treated any kind of way, people grumble and complain, while they go along with whatever others wants them to do in the hopes that others will love, accept, or give them their approval. Yet, by going along to get along with people who mistreat us, we are ensuring that they will continue to mistreat us.

The Role of Fear
As Negative Reinforcement

Fear Increases Undesirable Behavior

In the discussion above about reinforcement, only positive reinforcement was mentioned as a way to increase desirable behavior. Note that negative reinforcement also increases behavior. Fear negatively reinforces behavior and actually increases undesirable behavior in much the same way as positive reinforcement increases desirable behavior. The difference is that positive reinforcement increases behavior by adding something (e.g., money, hugs, toys) and negative reinforcement increases behavior by taking something away (e.g., fear, worry).[5] This is how fear plays a central role in the little deaths people experience daily.

Fear drives people to do all kinds of things they don't want to do in the effort to stop bad things from happening. The greatest fear is that things won't turn out as desired. This is manifested in a person's fear that people will leave or stop giving their love, or that his efforts will fail. Many people fear that they will lose control over themselves or their environment. So, people live their lives trying to make sure that these fears do not come to pass.

The sum effect of the fears, whatever the source, is that we sacrifice ourselves to the effort of keeping the fears in check. People try to control the feared outcome by failing to act in their own best interest, being commitment phobic, and being a doormat. These behaviors are all designed to relieve fear. Because acting out of fear often leads to the very thing people try to avoid, it is easy to miss the logic behind people's fear-based behavior. Just remember this: people do everything they do because they get something out of it.[5]

Fear of Failure

Fear of failure frequently keeps people from acting in their own best interest.[7] People often believe that they will do some important thing when they are no longer afraid to do it. What they don't realize is that the longer a person avoids doing something because she fears it, the longer she will fear it, and not get it done. This, of course, leads to increased fear.

How many times have you seen people who stay in a job, marriage, town, or any other situation they hate, even when more desirable alternatives are readily available to them? It would be very easy to negatively judge people in these circumstances because it can be very difficult to see the fear that keeps them rooted in place when looking from the outside. In fact, people in these situations often miss their own fear, typically attributing the reasons for their lack of movement to other seemingly logical causes (e.g., needing the money the job provides, staying married for the sake of the children, etc.).

Yet, if one took a closer look, one would see that the person fails to act in order to avoid fear. Often the fear is related to possible failure. Interestingly, the fear of failure is enough to keep people from acting because the fear acts as the negative reinforcement. As long as they don't do anything that might put them in the path of possible failure, then the fear stays away.

So, people are free to talk about quitting their job and going for their dream job. Similarly, they are free to think about moving across the country to experience a different culture or climate, and they are free to fantasize about getting the love they want – as long as they do not do anything to initiate the fear of failure associated with those plans.[7] We can see the power of the fear of failure all around us.

Fear of Abandonment

As with any fear, research also indicates that fear of abandonment is a powerful negative reinforcement.[6] This fear typically comes from the real agony caused by real or feared abandonment that occurred first during a person's childhood. Perhaps a person's father or mother left him to be raised by grandparents, or maybe the parents worked so much that they rarely saw the child. It is more likely that the father left the child to be raised by the mother alone. The emotional distress caused by the loss of the father may have been compounded by the child's constant fear of being abandoned by his overwhelmed mother.

Children often blame themselves when bad things happen in their lives, so it is common for children to believe that their parents left them because the children were unlovable. It takes very little imagination for a child to live in constant fear of eventual abandonment by the parent who stayed. Of the children whose biological families remain intact, countless numbers experience abandonment due to their parents' over-commitment to work and other activities that take them away from caring for their children. So, a fair number of children grow up feeling abandoned and fearing continued abandonment.

Fear of Abandonment as Commitment Phobia

Some people tend to act out their fears of abandonment by never fully committing to anything or anybody.[6] This includes spouses, children, friends, family, and work. In order to maintain emotional distance from people, this person fails to consistently follow through on his promises. Even though he may show up when it is really important (e.g., major events and activities), he does not follow through on the myriad promises and responsibilities that populate daily life.

He keeps plans vague and only commits to a course of action when he can be in control of most aspects of the activity. No one's needs are more important than his. He is always sizing up a situation to get the most benefit for himself. This person cheats on his spouse and neglects his children to meet his own needs.

If he does not cheat on his wife with another woman (or man - let's keep it real here) he cheats her and the children out of his time with over-involvement with other seemingly legitimate activities (e.g., church, golf, work, and other family commitments). This man is not going to allow himself to be vulnerable to the ones closest to him because she might leave him and take the children with her. This loss would be devastating. So, he protects himself by not allowing himself to become so attached.

Yet, from time to time he wonders why he feels so lonely and emotionally detached from the people around him. He grieves the fact that he does not have any deep emotional attachments with his family members or friends. He wonders why his children rarely seek him out and why he and his wife are living separate lives. In fact, this person has engineered the very thing he feared. If one were to place a mirror in front of his behavior to show him how he created this sad state of affairs for himself, he would have the hardest time seeing it, since all he tried to do was to protect himself.

Fear of Abandonment as Doormat

Then there are those who can be doormats for other people —spouse, children, friends, co-workers, neighbors — because of their fear of abandonment. [6] If they have it and you want it, it's yours for the taking. This person has great difficulty saying no to people about anything, often at the expense of herself and her family.

She is hungry for approval and acceptance. The only reciprocity she is looking for is positive appraisal and a person's continued presence in her life. She enjoys knowing that others think well of her (e.g., nice, smart, funny, or whatever else) even as others are sucking the life right out of her. She often finds herself in unsatisfying situations and wonders why people keep doing bad things to her. She believes that if she bends over backwards for others, then others will treat her well.

Instead of getting the love and approval she desires, she feels physically drained and used. She also feels disgusted because she usually has nothing to show for her efforts but being surrounded by a bunch of people who use her and take her for granted. Like the lonely man, she has engineered the very thing she feared – except she has actually abandoned herself. Again, if one were to place a mirror in front of her behavior to show her how she created this sad state of affairs for herself, she would have the hardest time seeing it, since all she tried to do was to help people.

Both of these people have allowed fear to determine how they relate to others. Instead of expressing their needs and asking for reciprocity in their relationships, both chose to hide their needs out of the fear that people would leave them rather than meet their needs. She wears herself out trying to please everyone hoping that they will want to give her something important in return. He wears himself out keeping his emotional distance from those he loves the most. In the end, they both are responsible for what they get – the lack of respect at work, the lack of intimacy and family life at home, and the lack of genuine reciprocity in friendship and family relationships. So, they end up unsatisfied and disgusted because of their own fears.

How People Can Save Themselves

Some People Are Not Good in Relationships

The fact is that certain people will not meet anyone's needs but their own. They do not desire to practice reciprocity in relationship functions, no matter how clearly one might state one's needs to them. One is especially likely to encounter people like this when one enters into relationships based on fear of abandonment. The commitment phobic likely married someone who does not deserve his commitment. So when he tries to talk to her about his emotional needs, this is brand new to her because this was never part of the original deal in the relationship.

Likewise, the doormat probably married someone who is either helpless or controlling. So when she talks to him about her emotional needs, the information is new to him too. It is likely that neither of their spouses is equipped to meet their emotional needs since this was not part of the original marriage contract. It would be like hiring an accountant and later deciding that you need a brain surgeon for the job. While it is likely that the brain surgeon could learn to read a balance sheet, it is far less likely that an accountant could learn to do brain surgery without a miracle.

Rearranging the Cast of Characters

When people decide to do things differently once they realize that they have arranged their lives in ways that guarantee their dissatisfaction, they might find that some people in their existing cast of characters can stay in their show because they are willing to do things the new way as dictated by the new star of the show. However, just as importantly, the new star of the show might realize that there is no longer a role for some of the key players when the plot to the story is rewritten. Often, when we begin to act in ways that maximize the chances of our needs getting met – rewarding desirable behaviors and punishing undesirable behaviors - the people who are not willing to meet our needs disappear with more or less speed. However, sometimes we have to deliberately remove toxic players from their key roles.

Embracing Fear

In order for people to create the lives they want for themselves, they must take the time to discover and embrace their fears so that they can stop acting out of them.[6] It is important for people to learn everything possible about their fears, including where they came from and what they look like in different situations. The easiest way to determine the source of fear is to imagine the worst thing that would happen if a person tried to write that book, left his job, said no to someone, or walked away from a relationship. The worst thing a person can imagine is the thing that fuels his fear.

Acting in One's Own Best Interest

The way for a person to break free of the fear is to deliberately act in her own best interest even while she is scared to death! Once people have mastered the art of acting in their own best interest with fear on board (that's really the definition of courage by the way), then the next step is to reward themselves and others for desirable behavior, and punish themselves and others for undesirable behavior. It might be hard for a person to get used to the new changes and fewer people in her life, but she will quickly find that it gets easier as she realizes more and more that life is not a dress rehearsal, nor is it meant to be high drama all of the time.

Summing It All Up

Despite the common belief that others or external circumstances are the cause of people's unhappiness, the *Ugly Fact* is that people ruin their own lives. While it is easier to blame sources outside of themselves, it is far more powerful for people to take responsibility for their own happiness. It belongs to them anyway, whether they accept it or not.

There are two ways that people ruin their own lives: rewarding negative behavior towards them, and falling under the influence of fear as negative reinforcement. The second scenario is often manifested as fear of failure and fear of abandonment. When people decide that they have had enough, start to act differently, and begin to expect behavioral reciprocity in their relationships, some people will stay, while some will leave, and others will need to be evicted from their lives.

Discovering and embracing the sources of their fears will lead people to do the things necessary to achieve the outcomes that they imagine for their own lives. Working towards their greatest goals with more reciprocal relationships, fewer unnecessary drains on their time and energy, and less drama in their lives will take people a long way towards living the lives of their wildest dreams.

Summary

The Final Take-Home Message

1.   The *5 Ugly Facts* are difficult to consider.

2.   Human behavior is predictable.

3.   Spread the news!

The Final Take-Home Message

The News

This book about *5 Ugly Facts* - men don't like kids, family members support alcohol and drug addiction, people do not change other people, domestic violence is an equal-opportunity killer, and people ruin their own lives - gave the reader information about five pressing behavioral topics and five social science theories. This book translated into everyday language what scientists know about human behavior that people see every day. Although the *5 Ugly Facts* presented in this book can be difficult to consider, they are important to address in order to minimize the unintended negative consequences of ignoring them. The goal of this presentation was to show the reader that human behavior can be predicted and changed, no matter how crazy it seems.

Spreading the News

Some readers will use the information presented in this book to help them understand their coursework better. Others will apply the information to those they help in their professions and pass it on to their co-workers. Still others will use the information to help themselves, and perhaps their family and friends. By all means, pass it on! The information is much too good to keep to yourself!

Bibliography
The Research Supporting
The *5 Ugly Facts*

Ugly Fact #1
Men Don't Like Kids!

1. Crosson-Tower, C. (2005). *Understanding child abuse and neglect.* Boston: Pearson Education, Inc.

2. Mintz, S. (2004). *Huck's raft. A history of American childhood.* Cambridge, MA: Harvard University Press.

3. Shusterman, G., Fluke, J., & McDonald, W.R. (2005). Male perpetrators of child maltreatment: findings from NCANDS. Retrieved August 28, 2007, from http://aspe.hhs.gov/hsp/05/child-maltreat/

4. Child Welfare Information Gateway. (2006). Child abuse and neglect fatalities: statistics and interventions. Retrieved August, 28, 2007, from http://www.childwelfare.gov/pubs/factsheets/fatality.cfm#backfn1

5. Nystrom, K., & Ohrling, K. (2004). Parenthood experiences during the child's first year: literature review. *Journal of Advanced Nursing, 46,* 319-330.

6. Coleman, W.L., Garfield, G., & Committee on Psychosocial Aspects of Child and Family Health. (2004). Fathers and pediatricians: enhancing men's roles in the care and development of their children. *Pediatrics, 5,* 1406-1411.

7. Bailey, W.T. (1994). A longitudinal study of fathers' involvement with young children: infancy to age 5 years. *Journal of Genetic Psychology, 155,* 331-339.

8. Roopnarine, J.L., Fouts, H.N., Lamb, M.E., & Lewis-Ellligan, T.Y. (2005). Mothers' and fathers' behavior toward their 3- to 4-month-old infants in lower, middle, and upper socioeconomic African-American families. *Developmental Psychology, 41*, 723-732.

9. Wood, J.J., & Repetti, R.L. (2004). What gets dad involved? A longitudinal study of change in parental child caregiving involvement. *Journal of Family Psychology, 18*, 237-249.

10. Horowitz, L.M. (2004). *Interpersonal foundations of psychopathology.* Washington, D.C: American Psychological Association.

11. Dubowitz, H., Black, M.M., Cox, C.E., Kerr, M.A. et al. (2001). Father involvement and children's functioning at 6 years: a multisite study. *Child Maltreatment, 6*, 300-309. Retrieved August 28, 2007, from http://cmx.sagepub.com/cgi/content/abstract/6/4/300

Ugly Fact #2
Family Members Support
Alcohol And Drug Addiction

1. Office of National Drug Control Policy. (2005). The economic cost of drug abuse in the United States 1992-2002. Retrieved August 28, 2007, from http://www.whitehouse drugpolicy.gov/publications/economic_costs/

2. National Institute on Drug Abuse. (1998). Economic costs of alcohol and drug abuse in the United States -1992. Retrieved August 28, 2007, from http://www.drugabuse.gov/ EconomicCosts/Index.html

3. Substance Abuse and Mental Health Services Administration. (2006). *Results from the 2005 National Survey on Drug Use and Health: national findings* (Office of Applied Studies, NSDUH Series H-30, DHHS Publication No. SMA 06-4194). Rockville, MD. Retrieved August 28, 2007, from http://oas.samhsa.gov

4. Rounds-Bryant, J.L., & Baker, L. (2007). Substance dependence and level of treatment need among recently-incarcerated prisoners. *The American Journal of Drug and Alcohol Abuse, 33*, 1-5

5. Hoffman, J., Fromke, S., & Cormier, M. (Producers). (2007). *Addiction* [Motion picture]. United States: Home Box Office.

6. Bowen, M. (2004). Bowen theory. Retrieved on August 28, 2007, from http://www.thebowencenter.org/pages/ theory.html

7.   Doweiko, H.E. (2002). *Concepts of chemical dependency*. Pacific Grove, CA: Brooks/Cole

8.   American Psychiatric Association. (2000). *Diagnostic and statistical manual of mental disorders (4th ed., text revision)*. Washington, DC: American Psychiatric Association.

9.   Nace, E.P., Birkmayer, F., Sullivan, M.A., Galanter, M., Fromson, J.A., Frances, R.J., Levin, F.R., Lewis, C., Suchinsky, R.T., Tamerin, J.S., & Westermeyer, J. (2007). Socially sanctioned coercion mechanisms for addiction treatment. *American Journal on Addictions, 16(1)*, 15-23.

10. Mintzer, I.L., Eisenberg, M., Terra, M., MacVane, C., Himmelstein, D.U., & Woolhandler, S. (2007). Treating opioid addiction with buprenorphine-naloxone in community-based primary care settings. *Annals of Family Medicine, 5(2)*, 146-50.

11. Dennis, M.L., Scott, C.K., Funk, R., & Foss, M.A. (2005). The duration and correlates of addiction and treatment careers. *Journal of Substance Abuse Treatment, 28 (Supplement 1)*: S51-S62.

12. Otto, M.W., O'Cleirigh, C.M., & Pollack, M.H. (2007). Attending to emotional cues for drug abuse: bridging the gap between clinic and home behaviors. *Science and Practice Perspectives, 3(2)*, 48-56.

Ugly Fact #3
People Do Not Change Other People

1. Comer, R.J. (2007). *Abnormal psychology* (6th ed.). New York: Worth Publishers.

2. Branch, M.N. (2006). How research in behavioral pharmacology informs behavioral science. *Journal of the Experimental Analysis of Behavior, 85(3)*, 407-423. Retrieved August 28, 2007, from http://www.pubmedcentral.nih.gov/ articlerender.fcgi?tool=pubmed&pubmedid=16776059

3. Zimmerman, G.L., Olsen, C.G., & Bosworth, M.F. (2000). A 'stages of change' approach to helping patients change behavior. *American Family Physician, 61(5)*. Retrieved August 15, 2007, from http://www.aafp.org/afp/20000301/ 1409.html

4. Pervin, L., Cervone, D., & Oliver, J. (2005). *Personality theory and research.* Hoboken, NJ: John Wiley & Sons, Inc.

Ugly Fact #4
Domestic Violence Is An
Equal-Opportunity Killer

1. National Center for Injury Prevention and Control. (2003).
    Cost of intimate partner violence against women in the United States.
    Atlanta: Centers for Disease Control and Prevention.
    Retrieved on August 28, 2007, from www.cdc.gov/ncipc/
    pub-res/ipv_cost/IPVBook-Final-Feb18.pdf

2. Stuart, G.L., Moore, T.M., Gordon, K.C., Ramsey, S.E., &
    Kahler, C.W. (2006). Psychopathology in women arrested for
    domestic violence. *Journal of Interpersonal Violence, 21(3)*, 376-
    389.

3. Fantuzzo, J., & Fusco, R. (2007). Children's direct sensory
    exposure to substantiated domestic violence crimes. *Violence
    and Victims, 22(2)*, 158-171.

4. Johnson, M.P. (2006). Conflict and control: gender symmetry
    and asymmetry in domestic violence. *Violence Against Women,
    12(11)*, 1003-1018.

5. Frye, V., Manganello, J., Campbell, J.C., Walton-Moss, B., &
    Wilt, S. (2006). The distribution of and factors associated
    with intimate terrorism and situational couple violence among
    a population-based sample of urban women in the United
    States. *Journal of Interpersonal Violence, 21(10)*, 1286-1313.

6. Schwarz, M.D. (2005). The past and future of violence against
    women. *Journal of Interpersonal Violence, 20(1)*, 7-11.

7.   Holtzworth-Munroe, A., & Meehan, J.C. (2004). Typologies of men who are maritally violent: scientific and clinical implications. *Journal of Interpersonal Violence, 19(12)*, 1369-1389.

8.   Dankowski, M.E., Keiley, M.K., Thomas, V., Choice, P., Lloyd, S.A., & Seery, B.L. (2006). Affect regulation and the cycle of violence against women: new directions for understanding the process. *Journal of Family Violence, 21(2)*, 327-339.

9.   Mayo Clinic (2007). Domestic violence towards women: recognize the patterns and seek help. Retrieved August 15, 2007, from http://www.mayoclinic.com/health/domestic-violence/WO00044

10.   Bensley, L., Van, Eenwyk, J., & Wynkoop Simmons, K. (2003). Childhood family violence history and women's risk for intimate partner violence and poor health. *American Journal of Preventive Medicine, 25(1)*, 38-44.

11.   Kaura, S.A., & Allen, C.M. (2004). Dissatisfaction with relationship power and dating violence perpetration by men and women. *Journal of Interpersonal Violence, 19(5)*, 576-588.

12.   Jackson, S., Feder, L., Forde, D.R., Davis, R.C., Maxwell, C.D., & Taylor, B.T. (2003). Batterer intervention programs: where do we go from here? Retrieved August 28, 2007, from http://www.ncjrs.gov/pdffiles1/nij/195079.pdf

13.   Petersen, R., Moracco, K.E., Goldstein, K.M., & Clark, K.A. (2004). Moving beyond disclosure: women's perspective on barriers and motivators to seeking assistance for intimate partner violence. *Women & Health, 40(3)*, 63-76.

14.   Chang, J.C., Cluss, P.A., Ranier, L., Hawker, L., Buranosky, R., Dado, D., McNeil, M., & Scholle, S.H. (2005). Health care interventions for intimate partner violence: what women want. *Women's Health Issues, 15(1)*, 21-30.

Ugly Fact #5
People Ruin Their Own Lives

1. Ventegodt, S., Andersen, N.J., & Merrick, J. (2003). Quality of life philosophy I. Quality of life, happiness, and meaning of life. *Scientific World Journal, 3*, 1164-1175.

2. Ventegodt, S., Merrick, J., & Andersen, N.J. (2003). Quality of life theory III. Maslow revisited. *Scientific World Journal, 3*, 1050-1057.

3. Sheldon, K.M., & Schachtman, T.R. (2007). Obligations, internalization, and excuse making: integrating the triangle model and self-determination theory. *Journal of Personality, 75(2)*, 359-381.

4. Mezulis, A.H., Abramson, L.Y., Hyde, J.S., & Hankins, B. (2004). Is there a universal positivity bias in attributions? A meta-analytic review of individual, developmental, and cultural differences in the self-serving attributional bias. *Psychological Bulletin, 130(5)*, 711-747.

5. Branch, M.N. (2006). How research in behavioral pharmacology informs behavioral science. *Journal of the Experimental Analysis of Behavior, 85(3)*, 407-423. Retrieved August 28, 2007, from http://www.pubmedcentral.nih.gov/articlerender.fcgi?tool=pubmed&pubmedid=16776059

6. Wei, M., & Tsun-Yao, K.(2007). Testing a conceptual model of working through self-defeating patterns. *Journal of Counseling Psychology, 54(3)*, 295-305.

7.   Steel, P. (2007). The nature of procrastination: a meta-analytic and theoretical review of quintessential self-regulatory failure. *Psychological Bulletin, 133(1)*, 65-94.

Book Orders

Items

Title of Book:
Number of Books: _____ x $24.95   _____
Tax (6.75% for NC residents only):   _____
Shipping: ($6.00 per book):   _____
Total Amount of Order: _____

Shipping Information (Please Print Clearly!)

Name: _____

Shipping Address: _____

City/State/Zip Code: _____

Telephone Number: _____

Payment Information
Credit Card Type (Visa, MasterCard, Discover, American Express)

_____
Credit Card Number   Expiration Date

_____
Name on Card

_____
Cardholder Signature

Please make cashier's checks and money orders payable to **MHS**

Mail payment and order form to: Mental Health Solutions,
P.O. Box 14413, Research Triangle Park, NC 27709-4413.

Book Orders

Copies of *5 Ugly Facts* are available at discount for bulk purchases, including fund-raising. This book is ideal for basic training in public service, human service, religious, and social organizations. Find more details about placing orders at **www.5UglyFacts.com**

Speaking Engagements

Contact Dr. Jennifer L. Rounds-Bryant at **www.5UglyFacts.com**